Coloring book for adults and kids amazing bear image for design

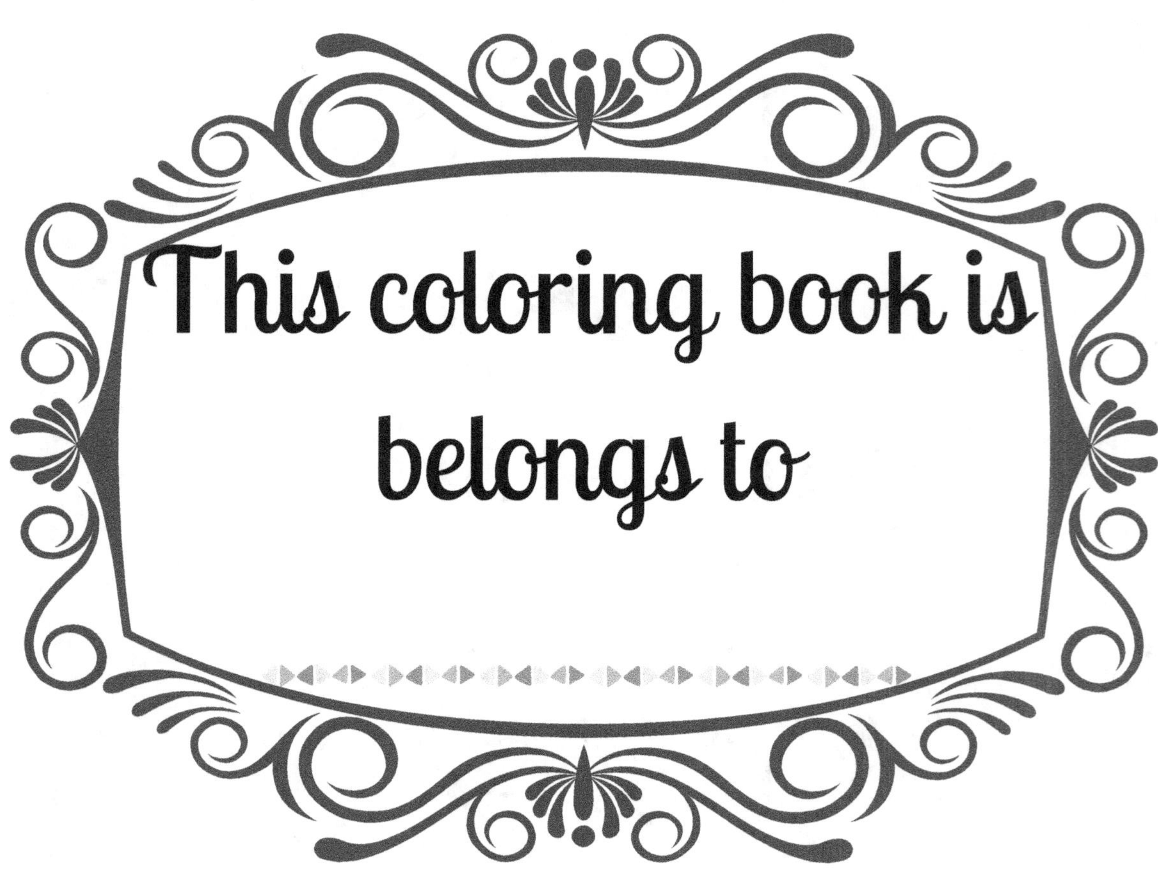

This coloring book is
belongs to

POLAR
BEAR

STAY WILD

www.ingramcontent.com/pod-product-compliance
Lightning Source LLC
Chambersburg PA
CBHW080037260726
48658CB00007B/2649